STRIPPER IN WONDERLAND

SOUTHERN MESSENGER POETS
Dave Smith, *Series Editor*

POEMS

Derrick Harriell

LOUISIANA STATE UNIVERSITY PRESS   BATON ROUGE

Published by Louisiana State University Press
Copyright © 2017 by Derrick Harriell
All rights reserved
Manufactured in the United States of America

DESIGNER: *Mandy McDonald Scallan*
TYPEFACE: *Ingeborg*
PRINTER AND BINDER: *LSI*

Library of Congress Cataloging-in-Publication Data
Names: Harriell, Derrick, author.
Title: Stripper in wonderland : poems / Derrick Harriell.
Description: Baton Rouge : Louisiana State University Press, [2017] | Series:
  Southern Messenger Poets
Identifiers: LCCN 2016039568| ISBN 978-0-8071-6552-2 (pbk. : alk. paper)
  paper) | ISBN 978-0-8071-6553-9 (pdf) | ISBN 978-0-8071-6554-6 (epub) | ISBN
  978-0-8071-6555-3 (mobi)
Classification: LCC PS3608.A78138 A6 2017 | DDC 811/.6—dc23
LC record available at https://lccn.loc.gov/2016039568

To Lashawn Robinson
for sharing wonderland

There are simply the Nows,
nothing more, nothing less
—JULIAN BARBOUR

I'm in love with a stripper
—T PAIN

CONTENTS

PIMPING THROUGH ETERNITY

ACKNOWLEDGEMENTS

I want to thank my dear friend Dave Smith for
selecting this book as part of LSU Press's
Southern Messenger Poets series and everyone
at the Press who had a hand in this collection.
Thank you to *The Louisville Review, Memorous,
Valley Voices,* and *Stone, River, Sky: An
Anthology of Georgia Poems* for being a home
to these poems. A huge shout to my three readers:
Kendra DeColo, Melissa Ginsburg, and James
Cherry, thank you. And I finally want to extend
my most infinite love and gratitude to April
and Drake Harriell, my eternal tribe; no matter
the "Now," I will always find you both, as
I always have.

STRIPPER IN WONDERLAND

17 Floors

not enough to hold all this   wonder   enchantment
       delirium sprayed on hotel walls   like
skunk cum   you coil my spine   like
stripper thighs on pole   slide down   stories wet
deep into adolescent dreams   I croak
again and again   I naked   except the burning
record in my throat on repeat   we   on repeat
a glass jukebox   we break   we never
break   dance with collapsing rain how it makes
this shit mellow   dramatic the way Hector weighs
outside lobby   clenching   a blooming Ruger
as if   it's your throat   just like   he clenched
your breasts on your honeymoon
how you confessed   I clenched your serotonin
there's a bullet with my heir's name on it he crouches
the Aztec warrior   plays the tlahuitolli like lightning
like electric   guitar

Pop Found the Apocalypse at the Bottom of a Bourbon

you flickered your tiny cop   flash
     light the dope fiend sky   eyes
flying saucers you swore you saw   a halo of orbs
over projects   said some thing came to you
in your sleep   rubbed whiskey on your belly like
vapor rub   asked if you wanted to go
down the wormhole   deep where porn stars glow
on sister planets   where the rabbit hole drops
you deep   in dark matter   shits you down
waterslide like   childhood dust burning your eyes
like beauty   you knew things
    we watched Alex Collier lectures for leap years
I started to see them too   look Pop   they're right there
at the bottom   of my bourbon benevolent   entities
orbs   radiant   disc   sleek   sexy   alien   love
notes in our funky ghetto blue   who knew
greys abducted the ghetto too   you knew
it wasn't just crap   circles in cornfields
for every gangster   was a twin   a galactic hovering
the earthling   like cosmic censorship   hypotheses
impossible

Bound to Relapse

tubes bound aged brolic to bunk /
bound to suffer /
bound to blues /
bound down on luck this evening /
if she lady / she one you sexed
broke / in another Now you bound
another broke / they broke domino
collapse bound your liver / bound
by bound / stripper crucify
your brown bound / until you believe
you're free as birth / bound in belief
you're flesh again

1000 Deaths

sub-howling woofers woof Brooklyn tragedy / the moon pops a fantasy
through this roof / this how gods lean / Mayan spacecraft pilot like
time traveler / abiding rap star like / tableau of smolder
the joint burns / a permanent print / on this leather
her abiding / a permanent print / on this swagger
you wished you stroked genie's lamp / with fire
shot down every werewolf vampire and Godzilla
in the goddamn galaxy / and tonight / thou shalt King Kong once more
once upon a time there was I / at a stoplight / with a Jeannie
and her Manolo Blahnik / booming "Heart of the City" / and you
riding envy / mechanically / like a Ferris wheel
like a goddamn bull

Rapping with Ghosts

translucent projection before me / you stand
awe-centered / a jammed flag
in my head / stinking of Bloody Mary's
garter belt
         how did you get here / find me
in the middle of this bedroom / we talk
I don't mention what he did
to you / don't mention the gun in my lap
for days / I would find him / I would kill him
then kill him again
        you said the other side
was orgasm before cigarette / said your kind butterfly
like eye blinks / I watched you drop stardust
from your mouth / blow flashbacks in beads
like bubbles

Bigfoot at the Edge of the Projects

it's wrecked it's brain 3 years and chomping /
      flicked suicidal raccoon and possum from its belly
apathetic / ever since it made that bad left
      then right / then abandoned
the stench of river and rock and waste / the concealment
      of leaves and tree and vine and carcass /
holy growl how it crooned the watchful night swoon
      in its day / how it invisibled right before
hunter and tourist and lens and moon and ghost /
      how its forefathers warned of gun
and carbon and neon and tattoo and smoke /
      how it climbed night for months of nights
christened its chops rare / wooly chest beating
      salivating at creation / what made such
angelic stench / how it found itself amongst angelic
      stench at the edge of the Hillside projects
enthralled / its mitts committed to a corner of Four
      Roses and refer ruins

Taxi to Airport to Airplane to Taxi to Hotel

baggage tremble in trunk like mafia hits / I want to swim
with fishes / Hades in turban / Allahu Akbar / engine burning
lipstick on eye / what do I owe for all this / what do I owe
you / reach for baggage like an aubade / the landscape
montage of monotony / déjà vu of voodoo / hoodoo
you love when I'm drunk in airport bars / love my filthy
proposals / that ass is mine / in a movie's time
love an airplane's stank / all its arrhythmia
love going up / how it pulls you under

Hades in dhoti / Om Bhur Bhuvah Svah / Mama-se
mama-sa ma-ma-kos-sa / the radio a rainbow's death
hum / what reservation / whose name / where
am I / the landscape grips your dome / like a yarmulke
I rode your head the whole way / I'm drunk in a hotel
bar / I'm praying East / I'm one you
from another incarnation / I ride the elevator on all fours
like a dragon / ride to your window
heave hades on these nuptial

Eternal Ethos of this Lobby Bar

write poem scraps on receipt
scraps / mortality right here / right Now
in another Now an oiled-up ebony scribbles Ebony
414 or what not / on a Burger King scrap
just like this / those hands tinier
than these knuckles / a dagger's length
from me / he's beating a business phone
muted / he's ready for a cab
and lonely body / he's eyeing knuckles
foreshadow like / how they carry wings
between us / how they gleam and scribble
and peel and stroke /
the way they unravel this world
sanctimoniously

The Investment Banker Stumbles into a Vegas Strip Club

pumped on too many / Mollys / too many / dead
lines / too many / nose blown
superlatives / salute / the morals / integrity /
the hedge funds / the benefits / beneficiaries / bonds / blondes
adorn Vegas boys / we all die ugly
in empty caskets / we all die and sign off
souls to men / women / children we barely know / take
what's reaped / what Harvard Wall Street afforded you
grim reaper / Candy Land Alexander / vanquisher
and ventriloquist / you got this / it's yours
like the Ackermann deal / yours / like the wretched tie
lights you / a tier below / rappers / atmospheres above
teachers / your hand raised / trophy clench
Grey Goose / glows / fiancé belly like /
platinum rapper like / you know all the words /
all the words / all the worlds
backdrop this pageant / and beauty bangs
your brain pulsar / like that time
you stumble out your last one

Bella (Vegas Psychic) Reads My Palm

Bella you beautiful / Bella you a disenchanted dollar / Bella
you wrapped in a flowerbed / Bella there's an Einstein
on your head / Bella I got bread and want to do it / Bella
tell my future / rumor my lovers / crochet constellations
all up and down my heart / chakra
all greasy with chicken / here my lips / all greasy
with waffles / I'm a pig / Bella
a muddy little cheater / Bella
my palms a body / all pink and petite / all flushed and eager
read them / they read a reefer / yesterday
silk camisole / yesterday a dirty novel / Bella
who my soul mate / you my soul mate / Bella
what color my children / who they mama / Bella
I know my ruling planets / her name Maria / Bella
am I rich in the future / are there hovercrafts

Novice in Wonderland

never imagine yourself not to be otherwise than what it might appear
—Alice in Wonderland

       starlight climb through anatomy of adolescent
       fantasy / United Nations nobility nude collapse
       this virgin bewildered / this not my first time
       I'm lying / always lying about firsts / once told
       a coworker I smoked from time to time /
       we smoked all the world's weed
       in my parent's basement / chain smoked
       until our hearts combusted beautifully

           I'm up to my naïve in skin / my watch
           in bafflement / my thrill in reprehend /
           move sheltered-child like / want to push
           all the buttons to all the games / reach for tokens
           like diamonds / keep cool in mine
           of sorcerer and spine and sparkle and whistle
           and everything / everything I've prayed whispered
           sin / this not my first time / keep cool

when made pole / defiled / pumped in public /
revelation drops hard / like her / I'm in love
not my first time / how to propose with thighs
noosing me numb / keep cool / when whispered
invoice / not my first time / incomprehensible invoice
when security semicircles / gang initiation like /
when I'm asking about credit cards
I've come too far

Magic City

you stole the universe unseen
the universe pretty complicated
constellations and slid them South /
didn't you / Atlanta /
you crackled sequined bang loud
it felt hush silent against hush reticent
those eyes leaning out faces
a field of archivists
tell future grandchildren eyes
back in my day we jumped
we jumped the fuck out faces
and died on a stage in Magic City
and didn't give a fuck /
didn't they / Atlanta /

you bleeding a green ceiling
caping untainted pretty
all this untainted pirouetting
above us / no one sees or sings
guns / all these guns poking
waists like stripper stings /
no one sees or sings
Hennessy / all this Hennessy
ride us drunk like jockeys /
and all we want are women
and record deals / Atlanta /
coffin loads of women
and record deals

The Rapper Leans into an Atlanta Strip Club

bright ghetto royalty   adorned   in bright ghetto manifestation
this earned   9–5 like   time and ½ like   time
flutters   a G-string   flutters   American coot
caught in a carnival   of bass   of fumes   of plants
and planets   and wet   and consumption

my man shooting the red pill tonight
he shooting a red pill off a brown belly
he shooting a red pill off a brown belly unfamiliar

outside   Midtown spreads its mouth
not yawn like   gator like   ironically
our guy   once blew a gator's head off   in Macon
he swears   he's whispering the story   to the ear
of an unfamiliar being   Diamond   right Now
he's rapping how he stalked   the reptile   how he braved
the bugs   the mud   the shrubs   how for nights
he heard the animal wheeze   beneath his bed   how its wet
scales prompted wet   dreams   of swamp   and sweat
and sweet   and beats   and boundless   wet

Interview to Taxi to Airport

who are your influences
don't ask about influences
> who not who you probably think
> who is / are / not who you know
> for example / who is nappy-headed
> tenement king inside leather cabin
> making us matter / brief moment
> collective dream gatherers
> punching shoulders debating
> whose future car it is /
> but better when who
> gets out and eyes
> my 100 pound body
> says something like
> not exactly
> but something like
> *lil man you wanna run with me /*
> hell yeah who / run
> these courts king
> run whatever you think
> I'm capable of running
> because when who passes the ball
> and that shot hits   who's
> *do that shit* approval
> makes me matter /
> when who says *I put money*
> *on lil man against any motherfucker*
> *out here /* makes me believe
> words alter worlds

rip me off driver man
all the money I never made
yours today / the negotiating
about my worth / resources
budget cuts / unsupportive
deans and such
led me to shower this city uncompensated /
not your fault driver man
but you love to talk /
not known for strip clubs /
go to Atlanta / you'll thank me /
American / *I'm flying American*
big bearded Black American
flying man / got kids to feed /
you got kids / then you know
the endless nature of their appetite /
right here works / *what I owe*
for the ride / the chatter /
take this change / cop shorty some candy
from a baby-fiending stranger

Make it Rain

we ascend   wheels at my feet   complex reminder
I'm a dead man flying   a whiskey-fiending fool
these wheels   threatening splinter   these things
go down   even if only   the rate of being struck
by lightening   it happens   what happens
when daddy don't walk through that door
and ashes flower a Mississippi cotton field
what happens   when daddy shows   in your dreams
or closet   outside your window   in winter
platinum haloed   tapping a bruise   a hip hop blues
electric techno   angel winged   it hasn't rained
for weeks   in Mississippi

      these things   I think   before
      whiskey   before   someone pushes
      the push cart   approach me   pusher-woman
      numb slinger   cash only   I know
      what you have   I know

buy the woman next to me a vodka   we rap
about reaping and sowing   law of attraction
the afterlife   she assures me   this plane
can't go down   it's impossible   like that question
of what came before the big bang

      we descend with awkward intent
      a voice leaps   from nothing   assures
      as my friend had   we won't die this afternoon

I'm committing my face to a window's sticky
watching life steam   and disappear   then steam again
and disappear   on the other side
rain barrels sideways   complicating gravity   just like
the angles which we flutter   like   the woman's hand
resting in mine   shaking   like   untamed bags
at our heads   the bleeding ice   in these cups

Twerk

my bloody heart / I'm teething it
ghetto squirrel like / dropping it
perished pan like / aneuryzed broom leaping
stripping / like meth-pumped obstetricians
he hustles / dirty hound like / foaming
at the heart / dragging
this void / broken like
martyred mockingbirds / like
suicidal twerkers

Lifetime of Lap Dances

so 96 Sadie Hawkins bump and grind like / this here
pure baby / this house of yours / my lap
      you live in it / like idol / holy wild
      hallelujah / this room sun spilled
spine stabbing / a breeze / pretty little
bed of splinters / you tornado tootsie
      ecstasy hocus pocus roll a quasar in my lap
      spin me galactic blue / you move
me cardiac flushed / all bent like
a beam / hunched over in this seat
      I'm snorting / your hair
      for granny / I'm burying
a shadow in your collarbone
I'm digging / dope-sick / satelliting / drunken fairy like
      you look down / at me / look up / at me / look back
      at it / this free will / all this / odd gravity / complex
oversoul we share / like surnames / like blood / this light

Bands

$'s bleed down my nose like coke   I'm a cowboy
in a candy store   dirty pop   philanthropist
drop it   on my gut   melee baby   got pastime bread
sign your name   on contracts   like zodiac
you beneficiary   golden outhouse
got bands baby   want college
got $'s   dead flowers   want a trust

bankers remind me   of your ratchet
your hunger   your requisites
the $'s your heart swallows
like claw crane   you reach   my pockets
1 hour at a time   watch me
flick $'s like dead   butts rotating horny spheres
stalking me   strip   tease robbing me
cents-less   say I'm your daddy   say I'm sugar

ASTRONAUTS IN MISSISSIPPI

Astronauts in Mississippi

why don't we cop rehearsed
country accents for a few weeks / snatch
a "sir" or "ma'am" or "y'all" from the dregs
of a past life / the dregs of a past life
contaminate this ether surrounding us
and me / hell I'm just captivated
and captive to this red earth / all this scorched
earth on this earth
constellations of cotton
fields in its atmosphere / I'm rolling
too green to shoot it whole / too Black
to be green / there's a Martian
beside the road rotating a hog
ceremonially / heat rises from red
and all I need is a place to land this damn ship
and Martian money / yes / Martian money for a piece
of what we've come in peace for
an anthropological undertaking
a hot plate with a cold narrative
a tasting zoo of graveyard and yardbird

Space Cadet

all these Delta mugs read you meager
home castles of Black bodies
from here   a Bermuda of bullets
debilitated   deaf uncle   bleeding
a lie out his crown   there's a woman
you forgot to marry   there
a velvet beach   you barefooting
Mississippi anatomy in an eastside bistro
you suspect   the world know you Mississippi
        bound   you belong   Americano to chops
stain like   Mississippi   land of speculation
like   that anthropologist   claimed a bunch of shit
about a bunch of shit   like   the homeless
beard wrapped in a bitter sidewalk
or   the warning wedged to this pump
hollering: *lighting that cig   right here   right Now*
can kill you   like the affair and beggar back North
the tornado   hollering   to take your happy head off

Gaia Smoking an American Spirit

Gaia's been drinking again   been screaming at Saturn again
the sirens howling again   my 2 year old crashing a car again
matter crashing   bending   outside a skittish window
    preparing to dust window   and bone and home
in the exhale   these highways hold hands
a prayer before perish   in the exhale
I remember Mississippi is suicide

                 in the exhale   those saucered eyes

dropping like power lines   in the exhale
    and Gaia's twerking   biting down on a cigarette
for the good times   buying a round for novice planets demonstrating
how to keep a calloused grip on the leash
how to yank parasites into place
how to scream them to repentance   deliver them to all fours

HWY 6

this birth canal of tourist and patient
    of Converse pushed on Salat
        this holy wormhole smoking against my window
            combusting like mosquitos and water broken moons

Baptist Memorial

surely people die here   born here   bleed here
these floors   surely catch desperate   Dear Father
Hail Mary   Stay With Me   cameras sniff
spirits   obliviously scouring   each floor
for familiar   tones   earth   tones
familiar   automatic doors   the waiting room
familiar   forms   the wheelchairs
the last time   2 cousins laid stabbed   wait   shot
no   1 stabbed   1 shot   all dead
what is it with a hospital silent enough to record a hymn
or her   eulogizing   she'd rather die   than birth this baby
in quiet

The Cowardly Obstetrician Delivers a Body

what makes a king out of a slave? courage!
—THE COWARDLY LION (*The Wizard of Oz*)

and he's not breathing / not breathing
and blue / not breathing blue baby of mine / no
ours / we made this / abracadabra blue not breathing baby
on a tequila sacked Saturday night / you calculated
the math / studied that calendar
said   *it was this day   that Saturday*
that night   you were on a tequila and rum
witch hunt / a stripper in your swagger
you were a horny homecoming king
and I was just there / you swear you were
just there / something for me to die in

but I / me / and my guides say
it was Sunday / after brunch / after I came
down from yesterday's yellow brick road /
remember I said   *honey fuck that yellow brick road*
I want to travel a dirt one with you
want to count flying things
on the porch of a shotgun
shack / remember I said   *let's wash our dirt*
down with champagne
and begin baptized / we are promised
like midmorning prayer / flooded
lungs at an ocean's floor

Crying in Our Cabernet

the ghost hour ghost
strangle us blue in the fear
no beer   tonight
this bottle decorated in dust
for this cry is a universe
down our throats
in darkness
in silence
we pour
whisper suicide grape
stain on chalice

we the sorry
pitiful shadows in moon-
smoke loathe baby
whole moon of it
while I curse
myself cockroach shame
planet of nobody
yeah
no show and snow day
I'm broken
blizzard about this living room
melted baby
freeze on a preemie's
blameless tongue

Mississippi Striptease

you tuck our honey munchkin sweetheart in
      a bunch of ghost-hearts valentine bless him neat /
           grow a dream from a root you thought croaked /

the news said people should watch the moon /
      it's predicted to honey bloodshot-moon us all /

we pump each other Mississippi stain
      on some Mississippi lawn / another Mississippi moves
           more damned than we understand / he's outwaited auctions

for some honeymoon shack / to feel
      begging beneath her scars / hatred brailled on her back

All Strippers Reincarnate to Mississippi

Christ resurrected Taylors and Chelseas chew
bubble gum beneath bible red kissers
blow Andrew and Brandon and Taylor
country kissers yoked in red-purple
clay colored bruised weathered cowgirl boots
line dance in a pickup truck's holy spotlight

them all racy country soundtrack matter
girls with Vegas and Hollywood déjà vu
memories whenever she circles / seduces
country boys belt buckle proud / country
spectacled Saturday Yee-haw whiskey hour bonfire
gives pulse to a county otherwise forgotten
otherwise engine and smoke and jean and leather
otherwise rubber and whiskey and seersucker and cigar

what to do when Madison starlights the line
ghetto ass drop Jackson's simmered lap / she will

and all of Mississippi will moon landing handclap
high five handshake catcall
celebrate her for their own private déjà vu
reminder of soulful opulence / of Louis
and Beamer and Cartier and Dolce
and she'll Christian
red bottom her way out those boots
into a bar of ghetto   music and ghetto
dancing / she'll wake daddy from a ghetto
nightmare where his baby shuts down a Jackson
bar / where she screams *I'm a bad bitch*
to a confederate moon at the 11:59 desperate
hour / she raises whiskey Rosé like
swallows the wealthy fingers that decorate her
by the county

Links Rd to HWY 6 to Jackson Ave

front confederate tag tells all I need to know
about the soul of this South / get it young country
bumpkin / make grandpa proud / push that pedal
like propaganda / like a hate you can't understand
what the hell I'm doing here / no permission /
who led me to this holy land
of hog / holy land of hate I'm rolling through /
same ole shit / different hate / this highway
reminds me of ghosts inside
grandma's kitchen / no / reminds me of uncles
punching each other in house party epilogues /
no / reminds me of calm before trauma
euphoria before a perfect wound

Unnamed Things

as I am a stranger here
—JAMES BALDWIN

the shot from the balcony of this blues bar reminds me of nothing
I remember of imaginative Oxford world building
in Milwaukee trap taverns a bunch of empty gas tanks ago /
nothing of this matter this hot matter cocooning me hot balcony mummy is
as I nightmared it to be / those boys in sheets are ghosts tonight
and even if not I'd still melt this American Spirit
slow as calloused fingertips on the bearded aficionado
plucking strings of some unnamed thing / tonight in this town right here
I'm an unnamed thing
observing unnamed whole / landfills and skylines of unnamed
all invisible slick flying biting things unnamed
islands of swelling flesh beneath southern gods
unnamed / dear city gods / why have ye forsaken me
lost ghetto dweller of gutbucket and lard-covered feelers
watch me not speak a word on this balcony
where are the writers you promised love making
on this balcony / antebellum architectured language barked
on this balcony / I'm all out of counting landmarks
and roundabouts / I'm easing into the unfathomableness of a monolithic
sky / just watch that boy's penny loafers scratch the concrete
with 2 left feet / watch that boy try and outrun
a bullet's devoted nature when released

Namesake

if ghosts are transparent strangeness
that walk through walls and sleep in closets then
you are not that / holographic haunting floating thing
hovering his bassinet in the ghost hour
having hitchhiked some paradoxical limbo /
I studied the outer space of his bassinet
for months for planets for comets for you
rehearsed the monologue until its language
became midnight's pulse in my dusty throat /
the paradoxical nature of faith is how it requires
faith / I knew you'd come the same way you knew
you wouldn't / but you were there
the morning he stopped breathing
and the moment / like they say happens / I moved out-of-body
and became watcher / watched my hands
and fingers lifeline him back / watched
how his face suddenly became yours / your names
eternally wedded

PIMPING THROUGH ETERNITY

Sunday

and declared to be the Son of God with power,
according to the spirit of holiness,
by the resurrection from the dead
—ROMANS 1:4

I'd only planned to observe / get in and out
anthropologic like / find bones and buried
blood of past violent moons / rehash
narrowly escaped burials / anatomy
salvaging politicking and midnight alley fleeing
to create a past moment from a future rendition
of a coward's embellishment / like the way
I'm full of shit when I hand to God swear
that night in that yard that bullet almost ruined
this crown / the way we're full of shit
when we hand to God swear
those threats from them boys that summer
didn't have us shook / you know

teaching college English only saves you
when you're teaching college English
but when you're playing tourist to a ruined colony
you may find yourself negotiating for life /
so when a body devoid of bullets ta-da poofs
glowing silhouette of mystification ghetto strolls
an interruption of nostalgic hyperbole
the fucking exact face you fed cereal to
you like to believe you've crossed over /
because you cried a funeral at that funeral
watched him lowered deep / clinched
an almost perished tulip like the born again end
of an almost buried hand

Monday

he's been on the wagon
for a moment sane we celebrate /
no cheers or toast or mention of being off /
we remember the relapse / the way
the diseased body does this Parkinson's thing /
like the time it took a whole song to land
that bottle to his mouth / he amends
for moments at his bedside / times we awaited
the call / funerals I nightmared into
a eulogy speech almost memorized / we celebrate
this miracle of moment and wagon
until he's agony flushed in forgiveness
overcome with cure

Tuesday

he asks how I knew mom was *the* one
tells of some girl from some cul-de-sac
born yesterday / I want to tell him
what his grandfather told me
the night I love-tapped an apartment door
love collected against my knuckles /
I asked my father about *the* one
a summer after the divorce / after he'd stuffed
his whole into an apartment barely enough
to convince him it wasn't a cell / but we never discussed prisons
just the impossibility of monogamy / how he wished me
better then closed his eyes and half-smiled / recollected
on half a dozen mistresses / a Casanova's half dozen
half-mast heart bleeding / half a lifetime away

Wednesday

we don't occupy the vessels we did
don't occupy poorly decorated
lower-level suburban duplex
don't occupy the 3 a.m. aftermath
of wounded weekends
don't occupy our 20s /
you tell me I'm still fly
as the graduate student inside
that broken suit like barren cave
praying spectators didn't spot
the flash of weekend flames
scattered about me like landfill stars /
remember I dropped science
fiction in your ear
while we Supermanned the dance floor
whispered promises
of small planets
for you / spacecrafts
for you / crystal homes
on mountain belts for you /
I believed so much in the future

we occupy the future like a church
damaged vows ago / smash cake
into the pretty part of ourselves /
I never told you I never believed
in invariable vows / the fat throat
of that preacher who made me
repeat after him / *I promise*
to occupy whatever space she needs
for eternity / promise to occupy
an accessible state of mind
to not go crazy

the future's nothing like I imagined /
when was the last time we leaped off a bridge
or discovered something new / invented
something to make us feel
evolved as convoluted characters
in ancient films about this very moment we occupy
and make promises in and cheers to
another future

Thursday

what do you believe the future of poetry to be
don't ask me about futures

Friday

writing the last poem is not like writing the best poem /
not drinking coffee in some kitchen during the paperboy hour
pounding some typewriter when some unnamed bird perches
outside some window / not holding hands on some long stroll
everything about pretty reminding you of pretty
grandchildren and pretty nights abroad / not camping
when some unnamed exquisite thing eats pretty out your hand /
not fish scale reflections off water pretty enough to see granny
on its floor / not winter spreading snow pretty outside a cabin /
no / it's more like standing in a morgue of Black bodies /
like the cold tongue across the gut of your throat / like realizing
they all have your pretty face

Saturday

I'm sliding my arm into the velvet guts of a blazer I hadn't worn
since last Saturday / I've been stalking
strip clubs again / been robbing my 401k
been searching for life
changing lap dances again / word is
Gaia's shutting down her last stage
tonight / I'm making sure I'm remembered
in the pantheon of strip club patrons
I'm hall of famed future etched into history
my throne properly preserved /
my children's children will visit
historical museums of garment removal
to find a wax figurine of me
near the stage exhibit / arm stretched
eagerly clutching a single dollar
like an equation that cures

I'm sliding my legs into the polyester belly of slacks I hadn't worn
since last Friday / grabbed a coffee
and contemplated the worth of retirement
without stages to house my IRA scratch
without champagne rooms to house my groove
without a future to fall in love with

I'm searching for a pantheon of stripper songs
nodding to the bass of my own nostalgia
the scratch of my own want / I'm ordering
a strong drink with a weak undertone
committing all my shallow
to this very monumental moment /
imagine it this way /
a middle-aged professor walks into a strip club
on the last day in the last hour at the last place
strip clubs will ever exist / soon they'll be a thing of the past
like dinosaurs and profiling
like his velvet blazer and polyester slacks
they'll find themselves buried
in the backyard of barbaric folktales
when men roamed the world aimlessly
looking for some body naked to beautify
some bewitching body to bury
in a drink and a dollar and a dream

Future Self Rapping to Present Self about the Past

you always assumed it was some divine entity
when you heard the bass in your ear
thought you'd been chosen
even though you never believed in God
remained confused about how a cynic
could receive the high whisper
aware of the contradiction in your thinking /
like how do you only believe in something
when it saves you / like from the flash
when you sprinted and pleaded *God*
don't let me die in this ghetto
I heard you / remember those sheets
she screamed / you were held prayer like
she pleaded *stay the night this time*
he's not coming home / but he did
not before something pulled you
out that door / some blue-eyed angel
refusing to watch you die an adulterer /
look / I'm not here to make you feel like shit
or take all the credit / just remember
the next time you running around believing
you the embodiment of God
not acknowledging me in all your chaos
I'll be watching like a gambler / compulsively
like a high-strung shepherd

Meditation for Gaia *(Strip Her)*

forgive me for dead butts and cans
records I sailed out sedan windows
flowerbeds and anthills I fucked up /
compromised contagion and personal gain
prayers / times I cursed your obscure body /
for non-recycled plastic and urine-laced oceans
making irresponsible love in urine-laced oceans /
for drunking the soil after someone's repass
tree pull-ups until a convulsing branch severs

That Space Bending Baby Making Moment

the afroed spaceman wants to share a tremble or 2
    with source and soul willing to lose
        an incarnation or 2 or whoever
            is moved holy ghost good enough
                to make a baby right here on the velvet floor
                of this radical thought
                    who's dirty enough to love
              like back in time of touch and taint
            air moves in fat falsetto moan strokes
          souls crowd the pending time and thought point
        to document the unsophistication of touch and tremble
      irresponsible nature of putting mouth to flesh
like some wild zoo-caged or museum-archived beast incapable of curbing
    "I" the act of ancestors who tried bombing themselves into smithereens

Fogging the Time Machine Windows

lift off baby / we lifted off lifetimes
building to this boundary of bliss / we taking off
this continuum / taking off / gravity / taking off
limitation / taking off death / lift off
your cool / apprehension / doubt / fear /
no perfect way to land in yesterday /
no parallel parking in a parallel universe

take off / the fantasy / take it off /
contaminated romance definitions / years
you found yourself molested in dragons / make it right
all things right / nights we ruined ourselves
in hotel slaughterhouses / right
mornings we collected limbs
like roadside litter / right

lift off / peace and love hyperbole /
park it in San Francisco / spacesuits off
we come in love / come in you / come in truth / future
freaks come in time machines / wormhole strippers
baby-making enlighteners / take us to your leader
your ghettos / your mothers / your record stores
your state capitals / your strip clubs

there's a future in our future /
dope place we can land / whole gardens
of love in that landing / take off
you / I'm pushing this pedal / firing levers / take off
1980 / mommy's pushing me out blue / take off
2040 / my baby's pushing a stroller / take off / lift off
take off / mommy's clothes daddy / 1979 / a good time
start the whole motherfucking thing over

Robots

don't take over the world
don't create an underground unlocatable mainframe
near earth's core or out there
in space responsible for reprogramming
humans hypnotized artificial by artificial
acumen created in someone's lab or basement
or Geppetto dream of Frankensteining an almost being
almost capable of reasoning and computer love /
once upon a time someone prophesized
programed lovers to be the next logical frame / wondered how
landing on Mars could change our loneliness
our fractured wanting / our lifetimes logged in
this irrepressible land of irreversible loathe

Mothership

for the believers

the doggone Dogon was right when they pointed to a constellation and claimed
we from there / rhythm in the universe of guitar and drum
and galactic gangster lean / eons of yesterdays whole eternities
of pimp and horn / time-traveling star voyagers and voyeurs
of earthling abomination stacked on abomination
pyramid of abomination on a planet hoping to make puberty
planet ain't even had the chance to churn a peaceful rotation
since earthlings found themselves addicted to themselves
the way they make themselves feel more meaningful
than conceded in the purgatory of truth

like Dogon we look up for deliverance / deliverance not foretold
in any bible / schoolhouse / street corner / rooftop / cipher
after hour / we wade in traumatized boulevards
up to our please in hope / to our waist
in patience and wait for light and beam
light us out these boulevards up
bliss this mothership flash the earth raise your cabins
up / pass the poison / hold hands / let's be loose
when beamed up / face to face with deep
cavern inside our deep yearning to locate deep meaning
from the offbeat of this home that keeps on fucking us / up

Ascension

was not like falling / or / romantically receiving a bullet
to the lifeline artery / pleasant fading into a boulevard
adorned in your high-deeds / you're not high
only what you become / watch the body
blow up beautifully / the stoppage of time / memory
crucifixion still / saunter through memory dense / bite
moments paused / access the old lover / how she sluggishly
sucks that cigarette / goodbye is a hole in your head / her contracting throat
a hole in your goodbye / the thought of suicide
a hole in your religion / pray memory holy ghosted / mommy
smashes a bottle / daddy's at the strip club again / her temples heartbeat
a hole of light / cigarette burns the scissor part
of your hand / embraces cut the past singular / hurt
becomes a wreath of light / the stripper haunts lavender
your firstborn is making first love

CPSIA information can be obtained
at www.ICGtesting.com
Printed in the USA
LVOW11s2017031017

551041LV00002B/256/P